(Thai) Land of Soup Recipes

A Flavor-quaking Expanse of Thai Soup Cookbook

BY: Ivy Hope

Copyright © 2020 by Ivy Hope

IVY HOPE
COOKBOOK

Copyright/License Page

My Loyal Reader, Here is a Gift For You

Gifts are always the best way to express gratitude. I express mine to you for buying my book and taking the time to read it. The gift is free e-books! This is the best thing that can happen to a book lover. If you enjoyed my book, you will love the free e-books you will get in your email. You will also be notified for special offers.

All you need to do is to subscribe by filling the box below. After I have your email on my list you will get a free book every day. Take this advantage to save money too. I won't only share the date when a discount or a special offer is available, but I will inform you in advance before it stops.

https://ivy-hope.subscribemenow.com

Table of Contents

Introduction

The soups in Thailand's cuisine taste amazingly flavorsome and have a luscious texture. While it is hard to keep up with the amount of cultural diversity in Asia, this book attempts to manifest the diverse soups made in Thailand. Most of the soups have three common yet inevitable aromatics: galangal root, lemongrass, and kaffir lime leaves that demarcate Thai soups from any other soup you may have had. The rich aroma and concentrated flavors of every soup are distinctive and delectable.

This cookbook contains 30 detailed recipes of Thai Soups with complete ingredients and detailed instructions that are easy to follow. Also, the time required to prepare the soup and the serving quantity is specified. Some of the quintessential soups in this cookbook are Tom Yum noodle soup, Tom Kha Gai, Gaeng Som, and Yen Ta Fo.

When you see the words attractive, tasty, and healthy together- they are the definition of Thai soups. This statement is no myth. Learn to make these highly nutritious and healthy soups that are a great dish for your family and can be made on Sundays when you do not want to put much effort into making a scrumptious and stomach fulfilling meal. You can now bring the Thai street food alive in your home by trying out these mind-blowing and yummy soup recipes from our Thai cookbook!

Points to Note:

1. Fish sauce can be replaced by soy sauce or salt- add it in the last to avoid over-salting your soup.

2. Thai red curry paste is best when you make them fresh at home, but they are available in the markets as well.

3. If you buy canned coconut milk, do not forget to dilute it to normal consistency (most of the time, you will have to dilute it to half the amount).

4. If you do not get Thai Golden Mountain Sauce, then replace it with Maggi sauce.

5. If galangal root is not available, then you can add ginger, but this will not substitute the galangal's flavors.

6. Add lime juice only after the cooking process is over, otherwise the soup may taste bitter.

7. Kaffir lime leaves have a distinct citrusy flavor that could be replaced by lime zest, bay leaves (for soups especially), or lemon thyme.

8. Always use only the white bottom part of the lemongrass stalk.

9. Most of the ingredients can be found in Asian supermarkets.

10. The dishes can be interchanged with the type of proteins used- Gai is chicken, Goong is prawns, Moo is pork, and Pla is fish.

11. All the animal-based broth can be replaced with vegetable stock.

Tom Yum Noodle Soup

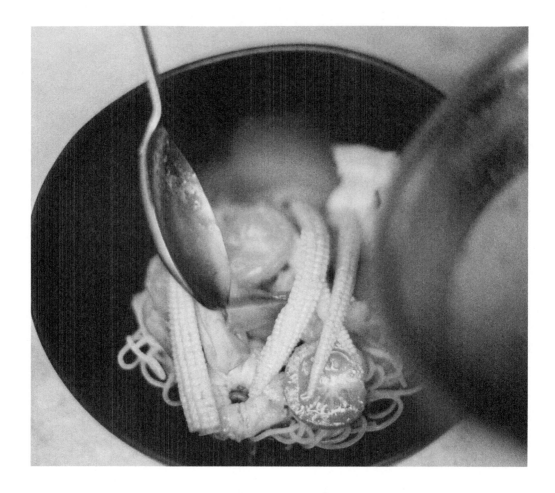

This is hands-down one of the best Thai dishes. There is a myriad of variations in Tom Yum Soup, and the most admirable version is the one with noodles, chicken, and shrimps. This taste-bud tantalizer can be created in a mere twenty minutes! This spicy and tangy creation can also be a one-pot dish. Get a flavor-blast from the multiple rich aromatics boiled together to represent the ultimate flavor of Thailand. Check out the recipe now!

Ingredients:

- 6-8 medium-sized shrimps shelled and deveined
- 2 oz thinly sliced chicken
- 1 ½ cups of water
- 6-7 slices of 2-inch long galangal (a ginger-like rhizome)
- 5-6 bird's eye chilies pounded (or any other spicy red chili)
- 1 stalk lemongrass- bottom white part pounded
- 3.5 oz tomato cut into wedges
- 2 garlic cloves
- 4 kaffir lime leaves (remove the midrib)
- 2 ½ tablespoons of Nam Prik Pao (Thai chili paste)
- 3.5 oz of mushrooms chopped (oyster, button or straw)
- ¼ cup of lime juice
- 2-3 tablespoons of fish sauce to taste
- Salt, to taste
- 14 oz of boiled noodles (egg, soba or instant)
- 3-4 Cilantro leaves for garnish

Preparation time: 20 minutes

Serving Size: 2

Instructions:

1. In a pan, add water and bring it to a boil while adding lemongrass, kaffir lime, galangal, tomato, and garlic.

2. Bring the flame to medium-low and add shrimps, mushroom, and chicken.

3. Add the pounded chilies and Nam Prik Pao and stir well for a spicy flavor profile.

4. Cover with a lid and simmer for around 3-5 minutes until the shrimps and chicken are cooked.

5. Turn off the gas and add the lime juice, fish sauce, and salt to get a sour, salty, and tangy flavor.

6. In a bowl of cooked noodles, pour the soup and garnish with cilantro.

Bone Soup with Rice

Bone soup with rice is a comfort food of Thailand, where they cook everything in one pot. The soup broth and the rice are cooked together. The soup has a rich flavor and is very delicious. This soup is rising in popularity due to its immense health benefits. This simple yet complex-flavored soup is a must-try and is very easy to make. If you are sick, this soup is an excellent choice to activate your senses. In most of the restaurants, beef ribs' bone soup is quite common, but the soup can be made using chicken and pork bone as well. Start soothing your soul right away with this simple recipe!

Ingredients:

- 1 beef bone (or few chicken bones) of your choice
- 2/3 cup of Jasmine rice
- 3 garlic cloves minced
- 1 tablespoon of cooking oil
- 1 onion chopped (optional)
- 2-3 kinds of leafy vegetables (Bok Choy or Pak Boong)
- 6-7 leaves of cilantro- chopped

for garnishing

- 4 tablespoons of ginger juliennes for garnishing
- Black pepper for seasoning, to taste
- Salt for seasoning, to taste

Preparation time: 2 hours

Serving Size: 4

Instructions:

1. In a large pan, bring your bone along with a pinch of salt to a boil for a minute when grey crud might rise towards the brim of the water which you have to remove.

2. In case you are using chicken, then cook it until the meat falls off the bone easily.

3. Simmer for half an hour to let the flavors ooze out from the bone slowly.

4. Then add onion and some salt.

5. Now add raw (uncooked) Jasmine rice and stir for a short while.

6. Keep simmering it under low heat for at least half an hour until the rice is almost soft and cooked.

7. Now add the green leafy vegetables of your choice and cook it for another 15 minutes when the rice also gets completely cooked.

8. Meanwhile, heat the oil and fry the garlic until it becomes aromatic and add it to the broth after the cooking is done.

9. Pour it into a bowl after removing the bones alone.

10. Garnish with cilantro, green onion, black pepper, and ginger.

Yen Ta Fo (Noodles in Pink Broth)

Yen Ta Fo, a famous pink noodle soup in Thailand, is aesthetically alluring and is a fantastic and funky lunch idea for kids as it contains pork, fried tofu, fish-shrimp balls, and squid floating in a broth that is sweet and sour and less spicy. All flavors are ravishing and tantalizing for your taste buds. The dazzling pink color comes from the fermented soybean paste. This iconic dish is very easy to make! Here are the directions for cooking Yen Ta Fo.

Ingredients:

For Yen Ta for sauce:

- 5 cubes of bean curds-fermented
- 4 teaspoons of water extracted from pickled garlic
- 3 teaspoons of Sriracha Hot Sauce
- 5 tablespoons of white vinegar
- 3 teaspoons of sugar
- 4-5 cloves of garlic
- 1-2 teaspoons of fish sauce

For broth:

- 6 ounces of chicken stock
- 1 ½ cups of proteins- any of the following can be used- fish balls, shrimp, squid, fish cakes, etc.
- Tofu puffs- 1 cup
- 2-4 teaspoons of garlic oil
- 2 cups of vegetables like spinach (use water morning glory for more authenticity)
- ½ tablespoon soy sauce
- 12 oz of Cooked noodles- any type
- ¼ teaspoon salt
- ½ teaspoon sugar
- Cilantro- 7-8 leaves for garnish
- White pepper, to taste

Preparation time: 40 minutes

Serving Size: 4

Instructions:

1. Mix all the ingredients for Yen Ta Fo sauce by blending them.

2. Simmer for 4-5 minutes on a pan until all the components are thoroughly cooked.

3. Bring the chicken stock to a boil and add all the seasonings and proteins.

4. Add tofu, fish balls, and vegetables in the last 2-3 minutes of simmering.

5. When the vegetables look cooked (and wilted), turn off the heat source.

6. For assembling all the key components, in a bowl, first, add 4-5 teaspoons of Yen Ta Fo sauce and a dash of garlic oil.

7. Add in the broth and garnish with cilantro.

Guay Tiew Ruea (Boat Noodles)

The name can be broken down into "Guay Tiew" which means noodles (and it can be any type of noodles- there are many varieties in Thailand) and "Ruea" which means boat. Traditionally, this soup was being made and served on the spot in floating boats which is why Guay Tiew Ruea is named "Boat Noodles". Many street food shops and boat vendors in Thailand make the Boat Noodles by thickening, enriching, and flavoring it with pig's blood. If you are not comfortable with using pig's blood, then you can substitute it with coconut milk. There exists a myriad of elements that go into this dish giving the noodle-soup a strong whiff of complex flavors. Follow these Instructions to create this iconic dish!

Ingredients:

- 2 pounds of pork bones (you also can use beef or veal bones)
- 2-3 white onions
- 6 cloves of large garlic
- 2 cilantro roots
- The top (white) part of 1 lemongrass
- Two 4-inches-long pandan leaves tied in a knot
- 3 pieces of star anise
- 3-4 of 8-inches-long galangal
- 2 cinnamon sticks
- 2 teaspoons of toasted coriander seeds
- 2 kaffir lime leaves
- 2-4 teaspoons of white peppercorns for seasoning
- 10 ounces of packet beef balls
- 1.3 ounces of beef blood (or pork blood)
- 1 pound of cooked noodles
- 1 cup bean sprouts
- 1 cup bok choy (or any other vegetables)
- ½ cup light soy sauce
- 1 teaspoon dark soy sauce
- 1 tablespoon yellow soybean paste (tao jiew)
- 2 teaspoons of white vinegar
- 6 bird's-eye chilies chopped
- 4 teaspoons of fried garlic
- 2 tablespoons of Garlic oil
- ½ tablespoon rock sugar

- Salt to taste

Preparation time: 30 minutes

Serving Size: 4

Instructions:

1. Blanch the bones in 6-8 cups of cold water and medium heat for 45 minutes to skim off the crud floating on top.

2. Reduce the heat to low and add all the spices and aromatics: onions, garlic, cilantro roots, lemongrass, pandan leaves, star anise, cinnamon, coriander seeds, kaffir lime leaves, galangal, rock sugar and peppercorns along with the soy sauces and the soybean paste.

3. Cook in low heat for 1 hour until the bones become tender.

4. Then strain everything from the broth- shred the meat out of its bone and re-use it.

5. Add in meatballs and heat until the meat is cooked.

6. Test the salt level- if it is less, add more salt, if it is more then stir and dilute the broth. (Remember that the noodles and the vegetables do not have any salt content, so add salt in a mindful way)

7. Add the beef blood to the pan slowly while stirring continuously to avoid coagulation and clumping of the blood. The more you add, the richer the broth becomes. Or add coconut milk for thickening and enriching the broth.

8. After stirring for another minute, turn off the gas.

9. In four bowls, place the cooked noodles (make it slightly undercooked if you want, since the hot broth will continue cooking the noodles) along with bok choy and bean sprouts.

10. Add some garlic oil to prevent the noodles from sticking to each other.

11. Pour in a mixture of chopped chilies and vinegar as per your spice preference.

12. Add the broth to the noodles and garnish with fried onions and cilantro.

Baa Mee Moo Daeng (Egg Noodle with Roasted Pork)

The roasted pork is red pork which can be barbecued according to your liking. This recipe is a definite hit as the smoky aroma of the pork resonates with the chewy al dente egg noodles to give you a mesmerizing flavor-packed bite. It is one of the favorite noodle dishes in Thailand and many have the dry version of this dish without the soup which can be prepared in just 20 minutes. The word "Baa Mee" refers to the egg noodles while "Moo Daeng" is the red barbecue pork part of the dish. The highlight of this dish is the fried garlic which is topped over the noodle-soup. Here are the steps to make this fancy soup!

Ingredients:

For the broth:

- Any bone part of pork- 1 (chopped)
- 3 carrots- diced
- 16 cups of water
- 1 teaspoon of rock sugar
- 2 ½ tablespoons of soy sauce
- 2 ½ tablespoons of fish sauce
- 1 ½ tablespoon of black peppercorns
- Salt to taste
- 1 cup of meatballs of any kind (fish, beef, etc.)

For the noodles and garnish:

- 2 bundles of egg noodles (between ½ and 1 cup)
- 1 cup Yu Choy chopped (or bok choy)
- 1-2 lbs. barbecued pork cut into slices and heated
- 1 lb. blanched bean sprouts
- 2 tablespoons of chopped cilantro
- 2-4 teaspoons of finely chopped and fried garlic
- 2-4 teaspoons of white pepper for seasoning
- 1 teaspoon of lime juice
- 2 tablespoons of crushed peanuts

Preparation time: 3 hours

Serving Size: 4

Instructions:

1. Boil the bones in a pan for 5 minutes and throw out the water.

2. In a clean pan, add the bones and 16 cups of water along with the carrots.

3. Once it starts boiling, reduce the flame to low and simmer it for 2 ½ hours while covering the pan.

4. Skim off the scum floating and filter the liquid removing the bones and carrots.

5. Add the peppercorn, soy sauce, fish sauce, and sugar to the clear broth and continue simmering.

6. Add in the meatballs and heat the broth until the meat is cooked.

7. Boil the noodles by adding salt and oil to a pan containing boiling water and placing the noodles in a strainer then dipping it in the water and stirring it continuously for 3-4 minutes until it is al dente.

8. Blanch the Yu Choy in boiling water for 2-3 minutes.

9. Place the noodles in a bowl and add a few drops of sesame or garlic oil to prevent the noodles from sticking to each other.

10. In the bowl, place the bean sprouts, Yu Choy, add in lime juice, fried garlic, white pepper, and the sliced red barbecue pork.

11. Pour the hot broth over the noodles and garnish with cilantro.

Khao-Soi (Northern Thai Curry Noodles)

Khao soi is a yellow-colored curry that came from Northern Thailand. It almost tastes like a red or green curry, but it is a soup. This dish has been significantly influenced by the Chinese immigrants who came to Thailand, which is why the curry paste contents in this dish are different from other Thai curried soups. The broth is coconut-milk based and people use mostly chicken as their protein in this soup. The flat egg noodles hold up the rich, creamy soup and are best complemented with pickled mustard greens and a dash of lime juice. Let us get started!

Ingredients:

For the curry paste:

- 5 red chilies- seeds to be discarded then soaked in water overnight.
- ½ teaspoon of sea salt
- ¼ cup of chopped shallots
- 2" long ginger sliced to give around 5 pieces
- 4 garlic cloves
- 1 stalk of lemongrass (the white part)
- ½ teaspoon of turmeric powder
- 2 teaspoons of coriander seed
- Seeds of 2 pods of black cardamom

For soup and noodles:

- 1 ½ lb. chicken drumsticks
- 3 cups of chicken stock
- 2 ½ tablespoons of soy sauce
- 2 ½ teaspoons of sugar
- 1 lb. flat egg noodles
- 1 lime
- 1 cup of chopped sour pickled mustard greens.
- ½ tsp. fried chili flakes (or adjust to the taste)
- 1 cup canola oil
- 2 cups of fresh coconut milk (or 2 "15-oz"-cans of unsweetened coconut milk-dilute it by half)
- Fish sauce- 2 teaspoons (or adjust to the taste)
- 4 round onion slices (from one medium-sized onion) for garnish

Preparation time: 2 hours

Serving Size: 4

Instructions:

1. Roast the cardamom seeds and coriander seeds on medium-high flame for around 4 minutes until the room is filled with the coriander seeds' aroma.

2. Brown and charr the ginger, garlic, lemongrass, and shallots along with turmeric powder on a heated pan- do not overcook them.

3. Grind cardamom and coriander seeds until they are powdered and keep it aside.

4. Pound the soaked chilies (soaking helps the curry to get better flavor and color) after straining away the water along with the coarse sea salt for extra friction.

5. Once the red chilies become a paste, pound the ginger, garlic, lemongrass, and shallots batch by batch for better grinding results.

6. After forming a paste, add the powdered cardamom and coriander seeds and grind them to combine everything.

7. Marinate the chicken with curry paste for a few hours.

8. In a pan, add 1 cup of canola oil and fry around ¼ part of the egg noodles until it becomes crispy and golden brown and keep it aside for garnishing later.

9. Remove the oil until 1 tablespoon of it is left and add the curry paste and fry it.

10. Add around half a cup of coconut milk to the pan and deglaze it, cooking until the volume reduces and the oil starts separating.

11. Add the chicken and coat it well with the curry paste mixture.

12. Add in the chicken stock, the rest of the coconut milk, 2 tablespoons of soy sauce and a little salt to the pan.

13. Bring it to a boil, then reduce the heat and simmer it for around 20-30 minutes until the chicken is thoroughly cooked.

14. Cook the flat egg noodles according to the instructions on the packet.

15. After cooking the creamy broth, add in the rest of the seasoning- remaining soy sauce, sugar, and fish sauce.

16. In a bowl, place the noodles and mustard greens. Pour the broth, add a dash of lime and place the fried noodles on top.

17. Garnish with onion slices and fried chili flakes.

Tom Ka Gai (Coconut Chicken Soup)

Translating to "Boil Galangal and Chicken", Tom Kha Gai is a luscious and creamy soup that gets its flavorful highlights from Galangal, lemongrass, and kaffir lime leaves infused into the coconut broth. You can go vegan by eliminating chicken and using any other vegan substitute like tofu and replacing fish sauce with just salt. Enjoy this summery rich deliciousness along with rice by following simple steps listed below.

Ingredients:

- 1 lb. chicken- chopped
- 6 cups of coconut milk (if you are using canned coconut milk, dilute it to half)
- 3 inches long galangal roots sliced
- 3 stalks (white part) of lemongrass- thinly sliced after pressing to release oils
- ½ cup scallions chopped
- 2 white onions (small)- diced into wedges
- 2 tomatoes diced
- 8 kaffir lime leaves- split into halves
- ½ lb. mushrooms (oyster, button or any other mushroom)
- 6-8 bird's eye chilies- finely chopped
- Fish sauce- 2 teaspoons (adjust according to the saltiness required)
- Salt to taste
- 4 tablespoons of lime juice
- 2 tablespoons of chopped cilantro for garnish

Preparation time: 20 minutes

Serving Size: 4

Instructions:

1. Boil 3 cups of coconut milk in a pan on high flame and add the chicken.

2. Stir for a short time and add the rest of the coconut milk. Reduce the flame to medium-low.

3. Add the chilies, fish sauce, mushrooms, and onions. Keep stirring the coconut milk in one direction while adding all the ingredients.

4. When the soup is starting to boil, add the tomatoes and the kaffir lime leaves.

5. Stir until the mushrooms and chicken are cooked completely. Make sure the coconut milk does not boil too much- just mild simmering.

6. Add salt if needed. Then switch off the heat and add chopped cilantro, scallions, and lime juice to balance out the richness of coconut milk and serve it in a bowl.

Tom Yum Goong (Thai Prawn Soup with Lemongrass Oil)

Tom Yum Goong is a hot and sour soup with a very similar recipe to the one of Tom Kha Gai except that, here, coconut milk is not used, making it less calorific, gluten-free, leaner, and lighter soup. This soup is one of the best representative soups of Thailand and is available everywhere in the country. This soup fits into a keto diet. The unique peppiness and pungency are taken to the next level by including prawn stock and lemongrass.

Ingredients:

- Prawns- 6-8 medium-sized
- Water- 4-6 cups
- 2 Lemongrass stalks (bottom white part)- lightly crushed and cut into two
- 3 inches galangal roots sliced
- 6-7 kaffir lime leaves torn apart
- 2-3 roughly chopped bird's eye chilies
- 1 white onion- diced
- 1 tomato- diced
- 4 garlic pods- sliced
- 2-3 tablespoons of canola oil
- 2 tablespoons of Nam Prik Pao (Thai chili paste)
- Fish sauce to taste (2-4 tablespoons roughly)
- 4 tablespoons of evaporated milk (or use heavy whipping cream to make it keto)
- 2 tablespoons of lime juice (or adjust it according to taste preference)
- 1 cup of mushrooms (oyster or any other mushroom)
- Cilantro - one handful for garnish

Preparation time: 10 minutes

Serving Size: 4

Instructions:

1. Remove the heads and shells of the prawns and keep it aside. Devein the prawns.

2. In a pan with some oil, fry the heads and shells of the prawn until the color changes.

3. Add water to the pan and scrape of anything remaining of the bottom and mix well.

4. Once it starts boiling, reduce the heat supply to a minimum and simmer it for 20 minutes.

5. Remove the prawn heads and shells and add in the lemongrass, galangal, bird's eye chilies, kaffir lime leaves, onion, and tomato to the prawn stock.

6. Heat until the broth starts boiling, then cover and cook it for 10 minutes on low flame.

7. Then add the Nam Prik Pao, evaporated milk and fish sauce to the broth and mix well.

8. Add in the mushrooms and simmer for another 5 minutes.

9. Add in the de-shelled and deveined prawns and stir for a minute or until the prawn gets cooked.

10. Turn off the heat and add lime juice, adjust the saltiness with fish sauce and garnish with cilantro.

Gaeng Som (Sour Soup)

Coming from the Southern part of Thailand, Gaeng Som is a curry-like soup, which is cooked in all homes. A pivotal part of this healthy dish is the versatile and buttery green papaya that makes your taste buds dance because it absorbs a myriad of flavors and gives the soup a chunky, and bitey experience. Typically, it is yellow because of turmeric. One key magical ingredient is "Grachai" or fingerroot (this rhizome can also be used after being soaked in brine). To maintain authenticity, you might have to go adventurous and make this hot and sour soup super spicy that clears your sins in the first swig. So, seafood lovers, here is the recipe for your favorite Thai soup!

Ingredients:

For Gaeng Som curry paste:

- Water- 3 cups
- 4-6 red chilies (remove the seeds)
- ½ cup shallots- chopped
- 4-6 garlic cloves
- 3 tablespoons of fresh Grachai
- Turmeric- 5 inches long- sliced
- 1 teaspoon of fermented shrimp paste (or replace it with miso paste if you are not comfortable with the overpowering shrimp flavor)

For the soup:

- 1 medium-sized green papaya- remove skin and dice it or slice it
- 3 cups chicken stock (or fish/shrimp stock)
- 1 medium-sized fish (cod or any other type)
- 1 cup Napa cabbage- chopped
- 2 tablespoon of tamarind juice
- 1-2 teaspoons of fish sauce
- 1 tablespoon sugar
- 3-6 tablespoons of lime juice
- Salt to taste

Preparation time: 30 minutes

Serving Size: 4

Instructions:

1. Blend the chilies, shallots, garlic, Grachai, turmeric, and shrimp paste together with a little amount of water to completely submerge all the ingredients

2. To a pan, add the curry paste and stock and heat on medium-high flame.

3. Once it starts simmering, add the papaya, sugar, tamarind and fish sauce.

4. Simmer for 8-10 minutes until the papaya is cooked. In the last two minutes of the papaya-cooking process, add in the Napa cabbage.

5. Add the fish and cook it for 6-8 minutes or until the fish gets completely cooked.

6. Add lime juice after switching off the flame and add salt according to taste.

Tom Saap (Isaan Soup)

Being a signature dish from the Isaan region of Thailand, Tom Saap is a pork ribs hot and sour soup brought to perfection with kaffir lime leaves, lemongrass, and galangal's tantalizing flavors that flutter in your mouth to warm up your soul on a cold wintery day. The bird's eye chilies in this dish stand out entailing a pungent yet palatable taste. Check out this simple and fun recipe!

Ingredients:

- Water- 50 oz
- Pork Ribs- 25 oz
- 3 inches long Galangal sliced
- 5 Kaffir lime leaves torn
- Lemongrass (white bottom part) - 2 stalks sliced
- 1 Coriander root
- 4 medium Tomatoes
- 1 cup Mushrooms
- 1 handful bunch of Thai Basil leaves
- ¼ cup chopped Shallots
- 1 teaspoon of Brown Sugar
- Fish sauce to taste (around 1 tablespoon)
- 1 Lime- juiced
- 1 teaspoon of chili flakes
- 6 chopped fresh bird's eye chilies
- 1 teaspoon Roasted and powdered ground rice
- 2-3 Spring Onion finely chopped for garnish

Preparation time: 1 hour 20 minutes

Serving Size: 4

Instructions:

1. Add pork ribs in a pan containing boiling water for 10 minutes then discard the water.

2. Add a fresh batch of water and add in the aromatics- lemongrass, galangal, shallots, coriander root, kaffir lime leaves, fresh bird's eye chilies along with brown sugar and fish sauce.

3. Once the broth starts boiling, simmer it down and cook it for an hour or more, until the pork ribs are tender.

4. 20 minutes before the one hour is up, add tomatoes, mushrooms, and Thai basil.

5. Once everything is cooked, switch off the heat and add rice powder and lime juice.

6. Serve in a bowl and garnish with chili flakes and spring onions.

Tamarind Soup with Seafood

Power-packed with flavors that burst like firecrackers in your mouth, the Thai Tamarind Soup with Seafood is a potential fancy one-pot dish entailing flavors you never imagined. Surprisingly, this fabulous food consists of simple ingredients and can be conjured up in just a few minutes. The best part is that you can go creative with your choice(s) of seafood! Put on your chef's hat because you are going to create a masterpiece dish!

Ingredients:

- 1 lb. fish (cod, red snapper or any other fish)
- 6-8 shrimps (you can also use tiger prawns, scallops, squid and clams- just cook them in the last 2 minutes until the clams open)
- 4 garlic cloves
- 1-2 chopped red chilies
- 2 stalks of lemongrass- white base only
- 3 kaffir lime leaves- torn
- 6 shallots chopped finely
- 6 cups of water
- 1 tablespoon of tamarind paste (or ¼ cup of tamarind juice)
- ¼ cup of palm sugar
- 2 tablespoons of fish sauce (or more according to the level of saltiness required)
- 2 inches ginger- julienned for garnish
- A handful of cilantro for garnish

Preparation time: 15 minutes

Serving Size: 4

Instructions:

1. In a pan with water, add the fish, shrimp, garlic, red chilies, lemongrass, shallots, and kaffir lime leaves.

2. Bring the pan to medium-high heat and add tamarind paste, palm sugar, and fish sauce.

3. Cook for 10 minutes until the fish is cooked.

4. Pour it in a bowl and garnish with ginger and cilantro.

Tom Jap Chai (Boiled Vegetables Soup)

Do not let the name "Boiled Vegetables Soup" fool you as it ironically contains meat (and sometimes additional poultry) as a crucial ingredient to bring out the layers of taste and textures in the expanse of the soup. Pork belly is what gives the soup thick and rich flavor. The vegetables used are traditionally the ones available in the daily market on the streets of Thailand, boiled to give a myriad of luscious-mellow tastes, including radish, cabbages, and cilantro. This delectable non-spicy dish is rich in vitamins and fiber. Follow this easy recipe to make Tom Jap Chai.

Ingredients:

- 3/4 lb. Pork belly chopped into bite-sized cubes
- 4 cups of diced Radish
- 1 cup of cilantro chopped roughly
- 1 whole Chinese cabbage- chopped
- 6-8 fried tofu cuboids from a 16 oz pack
- 1 whole kale- chopped
- 1 cup chopped bok choy
- ½ cup of water morning glory- chopped
- ½ cup sliced carrots
- ½ cup of cleaned and roughly chopped mushroom
- 2 tablespoons of crushed coriander seeds
- 6 cups of pork stock
- ¼ cup of cooking oil
- 6 tablespoons of soybean paste
- 3 tablespoons of fish sauce
- 3 teaspoons of dark soy sauce
- 2 teaspoons of finely chopped ginger
- 3 teaspoons of palm sugar
- 1 tablespoon of white peppercorns- crushed for garnishing

Preparation time: 1 hour

Serving Size: 4

Instructions:

1. In a large pan, heat the oil and fry soybean paste, coriander seeds' powder, garlic, ginger, radish, cleaned mushrooms, and carrots until the vegetables start leaving water.

2. Add the stock and the rest of the greens- cilantro, cabbage, kale, bok choy, morning glory, and tofu along with the pork. The greens may look like a lot of volumes, but they will reduce in volume as soon as they start softening up.

3. Add fish sauce, palm sugar, and dark soy sauce.

4. Cook for about an hour until the pork is cooked and the vegetables have wilted in size and almost gets integrated with the broth.

5. After the soup is done, serve it in a bowl and add the crushed peppercorns according to taste.

Gaeng Jued (Vegetable Soup)

If you want to keep a low flavor profile and have something that soothes your stomach while being heavenly relishing, out-of-the-box, and healthy at the same time, Gaeng Jued is the right choice. Literally translating to "Plain Soup", Gaeng Jued is a pleasant and satisfying combination of vegetables, pork, tofu and glass noodles. This quick and easy dish can be made vegetarian. Check out the following instructions!

Ingredients:

- ½ cup pork meatballs (make it beforehand by binding ½ lb. ground pork into balls with some white pepper, 1 teaspoon of oyster sauce, 2 teaspoons of fish sauce and 2 cloves of minced garlic and refrigerating it to bring firmness)
- 1-quart pork broth (or any other broth like chicken broth)
- 1 tablespoon fish sauce (add more to adjust saltiness)
- 4 garlic cloves- chopped
- 1 cup of mustard greens
- 1 whole Chinese cabbage- chopped
- 1 cup chopped bok choy
- ½ cup of water morning glory- chopped
- ¾ cup chopped carrots
- 1 cup cleaned mushrooms
- 16 oz of tofu- cubed
- 1.7 oz of glass noodles or Bean Thread Noodles (soak them for at least 10-15 minutes in warm water before using it in soup and follow instructions on the label)
- ¼ cup of chopped green onions for garnish
- ⅛ cup of Chopped cilantro for garnish
- 2-4 teaspoons of crushed Black peppercorn for seasoning

Preparation time: 20 minutes

Serving Size: 4

Instructions:

1. Heat the stock until it starts boiling. Then bring it to a simmer.

2. Add the meatballs, tofu, fish sauce, mushrooms, garlic, and all other vegetables and simmer them for 10 minutes. Add the leafy vegetables in the last five minutes to prevent overcooking.

3. In a bowl, place the glass noodles, add the soup, and add a dash of crushed black peppercorn and garnish with cilantro and green onions.

Gaeng Om (Herbal Curry)

The green and herb-infused broth makes you appreciate every flavor entailed in the soup. This aromatic soup can be used to detoxify your digestive system and please your stomach. Here, you can relish every single component of the soup. Even though this Northeastern Thai curry does not contain complex ingredients, the flavor of the soup broth is spectacular. Make this healthy soup by checking out this recipe!

Ingredients:

- ½ to 1 cup of chopped chicken
- 4 cups of chicken broth (or other any broth)
- 2 stalks of lemongrass- white base part only- crushed then sliced
- 2 ½ inches Galangal roughly sliced
- 4-5 kaffir lime leaves
- 3-4 bird's eye chilies chopped (adjust the amount according to your liking)
- ½ cup chopped shallots
- 4 cloves of garlic- chopped
- 2 inches ginger- chopped
- 1 cup mushroom (any type)
- 2 ½ cups of diced squash
- ¾ cup diced eggplants
- 1 cup mustard greens
- ¾ cup Thai basil
- 1 cup cabbage- chopped
- ¼ cup of dill leaves
- 1 tablespoon of roasted rice powder
- Fish sauce- 1 tablespoon or according to taste
- ¼ cup of chopped green shallots for garnish
- 2 tablespoons of chopped cilantro for garnish

Preparation time: 1 hour

Serving Size: 4

Instructions:

1. Grind or pound lemongrass, chilies, galangal, shallots, kaffir lime leaves, garlic, and ginger to make a paste.

2. In a pan, start boiling the stock then add the pasta and simmer it for a few minutes.

3. Then add the chicken, mushrooms, eggplants, squash, and fish sauce and cook for around 10 minutes until the chicken is cooked through.

4. Then, add the cabbage, dill, Thai basil leaves, mustard greens, and rice powder and cook for 2-3 minutes until the cabbage becomes soft.

5. After turning off the heat, add cilantro and green onion. Serve in a bowl.

Jim Jum (Soup Hot Pot)

Thailand offers a plethora of hot pots. Jim Jum stems from North-East Thailand and translates to "dunk and dip". The main elements of this hot pot are the soup-broth, thinly cut meat, dipping sauce, herbs, and vegetables, which end up flavoring the broth (so, maybe avoid vegetables like asparagus, beets, or broccoli that will flush out a strong flavor or color into the broth). This exciting and fun feast is not only scrumptious but healthy as well. Create a mega-feast using the step-by-step method given below!

Ingredients:

Sauce:

- 3-4 garlic cloves (roast or fry it if you do not like the raw taste)
- 1 tablespoon of coriander stems (or use 4 tablespoons of coriander leaves)- finely chopped
- 1 cup minced shallots
- ⅔ cup of fish sauce
- 2 limes- juiced
- 1 green onion stalk- finely chopped
- 2 sawtooth coriander- finely chopped
- 3 teaspoons of palm sugar
- 3 teaspoons of red chili flakes
- 2 tablespoons of tamarind juice
- 2 teaspoons of white peppercorn
- 2 tablespoons of toasted rice powder

Vegetables:

- Bok Choy- ¼ cup
- Carrots-chopped- ¼ cup
- Napa cabbage- ½ cup chopped
- Water spinach (morning glory)- ¼ cup chopped
- Shimeji mushrooms- chopped- 1 cup
- Oyster mushroom- chopped- ½ cup
- Radish sprouts- ¼ cup
- Celery- ½ cup chopped
- Fresh baby corns- ½ cup
- Zucchini- ½ cup

Herbs:

- Thai basil- ½ cup
- Sawtooth coriander- ½ cup

Broth:

- 4 cups of beef broth (pork can be used a swell)
- 2 lemongrass stalks-beaten and sliced
- 5-5 kaffir lime leaves- midrib vein removed; leaves torn
- 3 inches long galangal sliced into a round shape
- 1 tablespoon of fish sauce (not- the dipping sauce is salty, so salt the broth mildly)
- 1-2 tablespoons of toasted rice powder

Meat cuts:

- Beef liver and kidney- ¼ cup
- Thin slices pork meat- 2 cups
- Thinly sliced chicken- 2 cups
- Squid or any other seafood can be used- 1 cup
- Any other quickly cooking thinly sliced meat- 1 cup

Meat marination:

- For every ½ cup of meat, use:
- 2 teaspoons of oyster sauce
- 2 teaspoons of soy sauce
- 2 teaspoons of oil
- 2 tablespoons of egg white
- 1 teaspoon of cornstarch

(pre-cut meat for hot pot is available in Asian supermarkets. If you are going to slice your meat, then remember to slice it very thinly in bite-sized shapes. Freeze the meat for some time before you cut it using a knife to get more stability)

Glass noodles:

- 1 lb. glass noodles
- Water for soaking the noodles

Preparation time: 45 minutes

Serving Size: 4

Instructions:

1. Make the dipping sauce by mixing all the Ingredients except the toasted rice powder that you can add before you start eating the hot pot.

2. Cut all the vegetables into small, bit-sizes, and arrange it on a large plate.

3. In a pan with boiling beef stock, add galangal, lemongrass, kaffir lime leaves, and fish sauce and cook for 5 minutes for complete diffusion of aromatic flavors.

4. Then transfer broth into a hot pot where the soup boils very mildly and add the rice powder, herbs, and vegetables.

5. Soak the glass noodles in room temperature water for about 8-10 minutes until they become pliable then cut them into bite-sized lengths. Then cook it in the hot broth for just a few seconds before dipping in the dipping sauce and slurping on it.

6. Eat the vegetables by placing their broth-cooked version in a small bowl and adding few teaspoons of the dipping sauce. Leave the herbs in the broth to keep the aroma mixing through.

7. Marinate the meat by mixing all the Ingredients for an extra flavor blast and arrange in a platter.

8. Dip the thinly cut meat into egg yolk for retaining the meat-juices before dipping in the bubbling soup for a few seconds until it is cooked. Then dip it in the sauce and have it.

Gaeng Som Pla Chon (Snake-Head Fish with Sweet and Sour Soup)

Gaeng Som Pla Chon is a perfect winter delicacy rich in aroma and is quite wholesome. Usually, the entire de-gutted fish is fried in whole and served as a hot pot. The sourness from tamarind and sweet flavor from the brown sugar dances together in a perfect combination to marry with the fried Pla Chon or the snake-head fish for a palatable adventure. Follow this basic recipe for creating the wonderful dish.

Ingredients:

- 1 Pla Chon fish- de-head, de-tail and gutted (you can replace it with 1 ½ pound of brine-soaked canned herrings, poached trout or catfish)
- 4 cups of fish stock (chicken stock can be used too)
- Oil for frying- oil required until the fish is completely dunked in it
- 3 tablespoons of sour curry paste (used for Gaeng Som)
- 3 tablespoons of tamarind juice (you can dilute the paste and use)
- 3 teaspoons of palm sugar
- 2-3 cups of vegetables like Chinese cabbage, water mimosa, mustard greens, baby corn, carrots, radishes, string beans, shiitake mushrooms, and other green vegetables)
- Fish sauce to taste (around ¼ cup would be needed)

Preparation time: 30 minutes

Serving Size: 4

Instructions:

1. Fry the fish in hot oil until it becomes golden-brown in color and is cooked.

2. Boil the stock in a pan and add the sour curry paste.

3. Add in the palm sugar, tamarind juice, and fish sauce and dissolve the components thoroughly.

4. Add the harder vegetables like carrots, baby corn, and radishes first and let them cook for 10 minutes.

5. Then add the softer green vegetables and mushrooms except for water mimosa and cook them until they become soft. Taste the soup and add more salt or fish sauce to adjust the saltiness.

6. Place the fish into a bowl and add the soup with vegetables.

7. Top it with water mimosa and serve hot.

Kuay Jab (Rice Noodle Rolls in Soup)

Kuay Jab is a rich, flavorful, scrumptious, and heavy soup. The rice noodles are "rolled" because as soon as the trapezoid-shaped rice noodles (dried) descends into boiling-hot soup, it curls into rolls. The typical street-food Kuay Jab is also made along with the innards of pork, including tongue, heart, intestines, liver, and blood. The hot porky and peppery broth is very soothing and filling. The other highlight of this dish is the thick rice noodles that balance the flavors well with a starchy taste. Make this fun dish by looking up the recipe!

Ingredients:

For the pork belly:

- 1 pound pork belly
- 1 teaspoon of salt
- 4 tablespoons of fish sauce
- 2 tablespoons of white vinegar

For the rice noodle soup:

- 1 gallon of water
- ¾ cup of rice noodles (trapezoid-shaped)
- 1 lb. of pork intestine
- ½ cup sliced pork
- 1 ½ cup of fried tofu
- 1 cup of bean sprouts
- 6 hard-boiled eggs
- ½ tablespoon of coriander stalks
- 2 tablespoons of coriander leave chopped for garnish
- ½ cup of green onion chopped finely for garnish
- 6 garlic cloves crushed lightly to release flavor
- 2 stalks of celery cut along its length (optional)
- 3-4 teaspoons of dried black peppercorns
- 6 tablespoons of soy sauce
- 2 tablespoons of dark soy sauce
- 4-6 tablespoons of sugar (add according to taste)
- 1 tablespoon of vegetable oil
- 4 tablespoons of five-spices

- 2 tablespoons of vegetable oil
- 2 tablespoons of garlic oil for garnishing

Preparation time: 2 hours

Serving Size: 6

Instructions:

1. Pierce on the fatty side of the pork belly with a sharp knife and cover/smear the entire pork with the fish sauce and white vinegar and let it soak for 10 minutes.

2. With the fatty side up, lay the pork on a baking tray and season with salt evenly over the surface. Cook for 40 minutes at 220 degrees in the oven until the pork is well cooked and becomes crispy. Slice according to the required length and keep it aside for later use.

3. Soak the rice noodles in a bowl of hot water for 10 minutes and then strain the water. The sign of it being cooked is that the noodles will curl into white rolls.

4. In a pan with a gallon of water, add the coriander stalks, celery sticks, garlic, black peppers, and bring it to a boil at which point add the five-spice powder, soy sauce, dark soy sauce, vegetable oil, and sugar.

5. Bring the heat to medium-low and add in the tofu and boiled eggs. Cover the pan and simmer it for 15 minutes.

6. Now add the sliced pork and intestines and cook it for an hour until the pork becomes tender.

7. Add more fish sauce and soy sauce to adjust the taste.

8. In a bowl, place the noodles, bean sprouts, arrange a few pieces of tofu, and two halves of the eggs and place the crispy pork belly on the top. Then pour in the soup and garnish with green onions and cilantro and add the fried garlic oil to taste.

Guay Tiew Gai Marg (Chicken Noodle Soup with Bitter Melon)

Guay Tiew Gai Marg has a slightly different preparation method- it requires tossing and toasting over a pan then the making of a noodle soup broth. Unlike its prevalent cousins, Pad Thai and Pad See-ew, there are extra sauces for deep-erupting flavorful essence. The bitter melon is a quintessential addition to the soup and adds to its health benefits. This yummy chicken noodle dish is a quick-fix and uses simple ingredients too.

Ingredients:

For the chicken:

- 1 cup chicken chopped into bite-sized pieces.
- 1-2 tablespoons of soy sauce
- 2-3 teaspoons of oyster sauce
- 2 teaspoons of White pepper powder

For the soup:

- 1 lb. of wide rice noodles
- 2 cups of water
- 1 tablespoon of vegetable oil
- 4 teaspoons of sugar
- ½ tablespoon of finely chopped garlic
- ½ of a medium-sized bitter melon- the inside pulp and seeds are removed and sliced to give ½ inch thick semi-circles
- 2 inches galangal sliced finely
- 4 cloves of garlic
- 2 Thai red chilies
- 2 tablespoon soy sauce
- 2 teaspoons of fish sauce for seasoning
- 2-4 teaspoons of white pepper for garnish
- 2 tablespoons of Thai basil for garnish
- ¼ cup of green onions chopped for garnish
- 2 tablespoons of coriander leave chopped for garnish

Preparation time: 40 minutes

Serving Size: 2

Instructions:

1. Mix the chicken with the marinade and let it sit for at least 30 minutes.

2. Pound the lemongrass, galangal, garlic, and chilies progressively until they become very smooth.

3. Pour the oil into a wok or a non-stick pan on medium-high heat and put in the chopped garlic and the smooth paste, fry that for half a minute and then add the chicken pieces alone (do not add the rest of the marinade sauce).

4. Toss and fry the chicken until it is completely cooked.

5. Add in the water and then the sugar, soy sauce, and fish sauce.

6. Once the broth starts boiling, add in the melon and cook for 5 minutes until it becomes tender.

7. Cook the rice noodles according to the instructionsand place it in a bowl.

8. Pour the soup into the bowl and garnish with coriander leaves, Thai basil, green onion, and white pepper.

Soup Neua (Beef Soup)

Usually available in a Southern Thai-Muslim street food, this hearty dish is the best fix for a hungry, and craving stomach. The densely flavor-packed and spicy soup is a must-have for anyone who is trying out Thai soups. The rich beefiness is highly palatable and is enhanced with spiciness and rich flavors, making you want more of this comforting, heart-warming soup. Let's get cooking!

Ingredients:

- Beef broth- around 5-6 pints
- 1 lb. beef chunks
- 1 cup of bean sprouts
- 2 onions- halved
- 4-5 cloves of garlic
- ½ of a carrot
- 2 tablespoons of cilantro stems
- 1 teaspoon of salted soybeans
- 1 cube of preserved bean curd
- 3 pieces of star anises
- 3-4 pods of white cardamom
- 1 teaspoon of black pepper
- 1 tablespoon of dark soy sauce
- 1 tablespoon of light soy sauce
- ¼ teaspoon palm sugar
- ½ tablespoon of salt
- Coriander seeds- 1 teaspoon
- 3-5 thin slices of 2 inches long fresh galangal
- 1 stalk lemongrass- the white base- sliced thinly and diagonally
- 4 kaffir lime leaves, torn and the midrib vein is removed
- 1 cinnamon stick
- 2 rice noodle packets (to give 2 cups of noodles)
- 2-4 teaspoons of fried Garlic Oil to taste
- 4-8 Thai bird's eye chilies- diagonally chopped (adjust according to the spice level required.

- 2-3 teaspoons of fresh lime juice
- ¼ cup of Green onions for garnish, finely chopped
- 4-5 leaves from one stalk of fresh Thai basil

Preparation time: 2 hours

Serving Size: 4

Instructions:

1. In the boiling beef broth, add the onions, garlic, carrot, cilantro stems, star anise, cardamom, black pepper, sugar, cinnamon stick, salted soybeans, preserved bean curd, galangal, lemongrass, kaffir lime leaves, and the cardamom seeds. Then season it with dark soy sauce, light soy sauce, salt, and fish sauce.

2. Add in the beef chunks and cook it by simmering for about 30 minutes.

3. Cook the rice noodles according to instructions given on the packet and place it in a bowl along with bean sprouts. Add garlic oil to prevent the noodle strands from sticking to each other.

4. Remove everything except the beef chunks from the soup broth. Add more fish sauce if required.

5. Add the soup broth with beef pieces and garnish with red chilies, green onions, lime juice, and Thai basil leaves.

Pickled Mustard Green Soup

If you are hungry and ready to make anything as a quick-fix while also keeping a check on your health, piping-hot, Pickled Mustard Green Soup is your go-to meal. Make this soup in just 20 minutes to calm your midnight guilt-free cravings! This simple, yet delicious soup has very simple ingredients and is a fresh and divine soup that tastes mind-blowingly wonderful without much effort! Wait no more to create this easy one-pot dish!

Ingredients:

- 4 cups of chicken stock
- Pickled green mustard- 1 cup, leaves cut into ¾ inches length
- Chicken pieces- ½ cup (or any other protein that you prefer- this is optional)
- Soy sauce- 2 tablespoons
- Fish sauce- 2 teaspoons
- 14 oz noodles- any type
- ¼ cup of chopped scallions for garnishing
- 2-4 teaspoons of white pepper powder

for garnish

Preparation time: 15 minutes

Serving Size: 4

Instructions:

1. Boil the noodles according to instructions given.

2. In a pan with boiling chicken stock, add the soy sauce, fish sauce, and the chicken pieces and simmer until the chicken is cooked.

3. After the chicken is cooked, cook mustard greens for around 5-10 minutes until it is soft.

4. Place the noodles in a bowl and pour the soup over it and garnish with scallions and white pepper powder.

Thai Dumpling Soup (That-style Wonton Soup)

If you want to eat something that is off-the-beat and also is a quick-fix along with being incredibly delicious? The Chinese-influenced Thai Dumpling Soup has it all. This is a fun style of making soup and can be made fancy as well. The soup comforts your soul while the wantons fill your stomach with a blissful taste. Create something scrumptious by checking out our easy-to-follow recipe down here!

Ingredients:

For the paste:

- 2 cloves of garlic
- ½ teaspoon of white peppercorns
- 3 roots of cilantro

For the wantons and soup:

- 1 ½ cups of chicken or pork stock
- 15 ounces of ground pork meat
- 1 egg
- 1 ½ teaspoons of soy sauce
- 1 ½ teaspoons of oyster sauce
- 1 teaspoon of sugar
- ½ tablespoon of soy sauce
- 2 teaspoons of tapioca starch
- ½ teaspoon of fish sauce
- 1 cup mushrooms
- 1 stalk of lemongrass- the white part of the base
- Salt to taste
- ½ teaspoon of sugar
- A dash of white pepper
- Wonton sheets- Around 20-24
- Baby bok choy- 1 cup
- Water- 2 cups
- 2-4 teaspoons of chili oil for garnish
- 4 teaspoons of Fried garlic for garnish

- 2-4 teaspoons of Fried garlic oil for taste
- ¼ cup of chopped green onions for garnish

Preparation time: 35 minutes

Serving Size: 4

Instructions:

1. Make a paste by pounding garlic, white peppercorns, and cilantro stem together.

2. In a food processor, add the pork, egg, sugar, tapioca starch, soy sauce, oyster sauce, and the paste previously made and grind them almost coarsely.

3. In a wonton sheet, add a teaspoon worth filling and make wontons.

4. In a pan, boil the stock with soy sauce, fish sauce, lemongrass, mushrooms, salt, sugar, and a dash of white pepper and cook it for 5 minutes before turning off the heat.

5. In boiling water, cook the bok choy for a minute before using the water to cook the wantons and place it in a bowl.

6. Then add in the wantons and cook them for 2-3 minutes and place them in a bowl.

7. Add the soup into the bowl and garnish it with fried garlic, fried garlic oil, chili oil, and green onions.

Shrimp Tom Yum in Coconut Water

Similar to the recipe of Tom Yum soup, here we have a twist in the style of cooking. We use coconut water as the broth to cook all the aromatics and proteins. The fresh, mildly sweet flavor of coconut water blends in smoothly with the aromatics and spices to give the final dish a beautiful fragrance and flavor. So, do not wait any longer to make this spectacular dish in a jiffy!

Ingredients:

- 10-12 medium shrimps (shelled without removing the tail-quantity can be adjusted)
- 4 Cups Coconut Water
- 2 Stalks of Fresh Lemongrass- beaten then sliced
- 2 inches long Galangal sliced
- 3-4 kaffir lime leaves with the midrib vein removed
- 2 cloves of garlic pounded
- 2 medium-sized tomatoes cut into wedges
- 3 chopped shallots
- 1 cup of mushrooms
- 6 teaspoons of Fish Sauce
- 6 teaspoons of Lime Juice
- 2 teaspoons of Nam Prik Pao (Thai chili paste or sauce)
- 2 teaspoons of tamarind sauce
- 3-4 chopped fresh bird's eye chilies or Thai red chilies for garnish
- A handful of cilantro chopped for garnish

Preparation time: 30 minutes

Serving Size: 4

Instructions:

1. In a pan, turn the heat to medium and add coconut water, lemongrass, galangal, kaffir lime leaves, garlic and tomatoes, and shallots and bring it to a boil.

2. Then add the shrimps and mushrooms along with the fish sauce, Nam Prik Pao, and tamarind sauce.

3. After the shrimps and the mushrooms are cooked (will take a few minutes only) turn off the heat, test the saltiness and add more fish sauce if required. Add a dash of lime juice and serve it in a bowl.

4. Garnish with chilies and cilantro.

Special Thai Orange Fish Soup

Thai Orange Fish Soup is an invigoratingly salubrious soup packed with a large number of healthy ingredients.

Stemming from the fields of Central Thailand, this spicy soup balances with the sweet and sour overtones to give a yummy and simple dish. The orange adds a new supple flavor to the broth that enriches the aroma and gives a subtle citrusy flavor to the soup for a blissful experience in your mouth and stomach. Now, you can make this soup by following the simple steps listed below!

Ingredients:

- 6 cups of fish stock
- 1 Pla Chon fish fillets (or use 1 ½ pound of herrings, trout or catfish fillets)
- 12-14 medium-sized shrimps
- 1 cup of freshly squeezed orange juice
- 1 teaspoon of tamarind paste
- 2 teaspoons of lime juice
- 1 ½ teaspoons of palm sugar
- 2 teaspoons of red curry paste
- 3 tablespoons of fish sauce
- 2 cups of bok choy (baby bok choy is preferred)- chopped
- ½ cup of halved cherry tomatoes
- ¾ cup of chopped green beans cut into 2-inches lengths
- 8 orange slices for garnish
- 2 tablespoons of cilantro chopped for garnish

Preparation time: 25 minutes

Serving Size: 4

Instructions:

1. In a pan, add the red paste in the stock and mix it well. Then add the tamarind paste, palm sugar, and fish sauce.

2. Once it comes to a boil, add the green beans and cook for a few minutes until it becomes soft. Then add in other vegetables along with the fish and simmer for 2-3 minutes until the fish is completely cooked.

3. Add lime juice and adjust the flavor. Do not stir the pan too much as the fish would disintegrate.

4. Pour it in a bowl and garnish with 2-3 orange slices and cilantro.

Thai Congee (Rice Porridge with Pork)

Thai congee is a complete breakfast package and rich in nutrients and starch for anyone to start their day off with a high note. Known as "Jok" in Thailand, this is one of the best foods to be taken when someone is ill. Thai congee is a rice porridge that is not sweet but savory and served with various Thai condiments along with pork meatballs. Add a zing to your breakfast by following this recipe listed with easy-to-follow steps!

Ingredients:

- ⅓ cup of broken rice cooked in water
- Pork stock- 6 cups
- 1 medium-sized onion- cut into halves
- ½ cup of chopped Napa cabbage
- ½ of radish
- 2 teaspoons of sugar
- 8 white peppercorns- whole
- 6 garlic cloves- crush for more flavors
- ½ teaspoon of coriander seeds
- Salt, to taste
- Pork meatballs- ¾ cup
- 4 eggs
- 2 tablespoons of ginger juliennes for garnish
- ¼ cup of chopped scallions for garnish
- 4 tablespoons of fried garlic for garnish
- 2 teaspoons of fish sauce to taste (for making it vegetarian, use soy sauce)
- White pepper powder- 2-4 teaspoons

Preparation time: 1 hour 20 minutes

Serving Size: 4

Instructions:

1. In a pan with boiling stock, add the onion, cabbage, radish, white peppercorns, garlic, sugar, and salt. Add fish sauce or soy sauce to taste and simmer for 20 minutes.

2. Add the meatballs into the soup and cook for 3-4 minutes.

3. Poach the eggs in the soup broth for a few minutes until the white remains stable but the yolk is runny so that it keeps cooking even while serving.

4. Serve by placing cooked rice in a bowl and pouring soup over it that contains one poached egg and few pork meatballs.

5. Place ginger juliennes and chopped garlic. Add more fish sauce if required. Pour some spoonfuls of fried garlic and its oil.

6. Add a dash of white pepper. Thai congee is now ready to eat.

Gaeng Tai Pla (Fermented Fish Entrail Soup with Vegetables)

Explore the new flavors with Gaeng Tai Pla, as it contains fish guts, including pickled fish bladder and kidneys, for giving a strong base to the soup. The best part of this soup is that it is very straightforward. So, start adding vibrant tones to your bowls by making this delectable soup in just four simple steps!

Ingredients:

- 1 tablespoon of Thai red curry paste
- 1 whole dried fish cut into large chunks
- ½ cup of seasonal vegetables (eggplants, mustard greens, etc.)
- ½ cup of bamboo shoots chopped into pieces with 2 inches length
- 4 tablespoons of Tai Pla (pickled fish bladder)
- 2 ½ cups of water
- 2 teaspoons of sugar
- A dash of lime juice
- 8-10 kaffir lime leaves torn, midrib vein removed
- ¼ cup of chopped fresh cilantro for garnish

Preparation time: 25 minutes

Serving Size: 4

Instructions:

1. In a pan with 2 cups of boiling water, add the fish entrails and stir well until the flavor diffuses in the water. Strain out the fish entrails to leave a watery broth.

2. In half a cup of water, add in the curry paste, mix well and add it to the pan.

3. Add the vegetables and bamboo shoots and cook them for 5 minutes. Then add the dried fish chunks, lime juice, sugar, and kaffir lime leaves and stir until the fish cooks through.

4. Serve in a bowl and garnish with fresh cilantro.

Gai Joo Khing (Thai Chicken and Ginger Soup)

Thai soup, "Gai Joo Khing," has a strong aroma and flavors. The soup gets its warmth and spice from the ginger and pepper powder. Make this soup to cleanse your system and comfort your soul. Freshen your digestive system by checking out this recipe!

Ingredients:

- 1 tablespoon of cooking oil
- 1 ½ cups of diced chicken (bite-sized)
- 2 cloves of garlic made into a paste
- ½ cup of ginger made into a paste
- 3 teaspoons of soybean paste (yellow bean sauce)
- 2 cups of soup stock
- Chopped shallots- ½ cup
- 2 teaspoons of thin soy sauce
- Salt to taste
- 2 teaspoons of white pepper powder
- 4-5 stalks of green onion cut into 1 inch long pieces
- ¼ cup of chopped cilantro for garnish
- 2-4 teaspoons of garlic oil for garnish
- 1-2 bird's eye chilies chopped or crushed for garnish

Preparation time: 15 minutes

Serving Size: 4

Instructions:

1. In a wok with heated oil, add in the chicken, ginger and garlic paste and stir-fry until the chicken is cooked through.

2. Add the soup stock, soybean paste, chopped shallots, and cook it for a few minutes (around 4-5 minutes).

3. Add in soy sauce, white pepper and salt to season and serve in a bowl.

4. Garnish with fresh cilantro, garlic oil, and bird's eye chilies.

Phak Tom Kati (Thai Vegetables in Coconut Milk)

Phak Tom Kati is a rich and delicious vegetarian soup. Coconut milk and vegetables complement each other beautifully. You can cook this dish with your family and have a fun-time by letting everyone add their favorite vegetable(s) into this dish! The herbs in the broth add a powerful and dense character to the soup. Make this soup in a matter of just a few minutes by following our easy instructions!

Ingredients:

- 1 cup of coconut milk
- 14 oz of noodles (any type)- can be replaced with rice
- 1/2 cup of fresh garden peas
- 2 cups worth vegetables that can include long beans, mushrooms, cabbage, tomatoes, bell peppers, baby corn, broccoli, and carrots
- ⅛ cup of chopped shallots
- 1 lemongrass stalk- sliced (white part only)
- 4-5 kaffir lime leaves torn
- 1 teaspoon of light soy sauce
- 1 ½ teaspoons of palm sugar
- Salt to taste
- 2-3 bird's eye chilies chopped finely (adjust according to spice level required)
- 1 tablespoon of green peppercorns
- 2 tablespoons of julienned ginger for garnish
- 2 tablespoons of cilantro- chopped for garnish

Preparation time: 20 minutes

Serving Size: 4

Instructions:

1. In a pan, bring the coconut milk to a boil and reduce the flame to create a mild simmering condition.

2. Add the aromatics like shallots, lemongrass, kaffir lime leaves, and green peppercorns and simmer it for 2-3 minutes after which add the rest of the vegetables except for green peas.

3. Before closing the lid for simmering and cooking the vegetables, add the palm sugar, soy sauce, chilies and salt, and taste for adjusting the seasonings.

4. After all the vegetables are cooked, add in the fresh peas and cook it for a minute or two until the peas are soft.

5. Cook the noodles according to the instructions on the packet given.

6. In a bowl, place the noodles and add them in the soup. Garnish with ginger and cilantro.

Thai-style Sukiyaki (Suki Nam)

Inspired from Japan's sukiyaki, this hot-pot dish is tweaked into Thai-style "suki". The main character of this dish is the sauce that carries an unfathomable flavor that helps elevate the aroma and taste of the juicy chicken used in this masterpiece. There are three versions of Suki: hot-pot, soup, and "Haeng" or dry version. This dish is a must-try as it has tantalizing and tempting flavors from the broth, keeping you hooked to this dish.

Ingredients:

For the suki sauce:

- 3 cloves of fresh garlic

- 3 cloves of pickled garlic

- 2-4 Thai red chilies

- 3 teaspoons of sugar

- 4 red bean curds

- 3 teaspoons of red bean curd juice

- ¼ cup of pickled garlic water

- 1 tablespoon of soy sauce

- 1 tablespoon of toasted sesame oil

- 2 teaspoons of toasted white sesame seeds

- 4 tablespoons for chopped cilantro

For marinating chicken:

- 1 ½ cups of chicken breasts chopped (add more if you like)

- 2 tablespoons of soy sauce

- 2 tablespoons of oyster sauce

- 2 teaspoons of toasted sesame oil

- 2 egg whites

- 4 tablespoons of tapioca starch

- The rest of Suki Nam:

- 1.5 ounces of glass noodles

- 4 cups of unsalted chicken or pork stock

- 2 eggs

- 2-3 tablespoons of sriracha sauce

Preparation time: 1 hour

Serving Size: 4

Instructions:

1. Pound the garlic, chilies, and sugar into a paste. Then add the bean curds and pound again. Add bean curd juice, pickled garlic water, soy sauce, and sesame oil and mix them all thoroughly. Add the toasted sesame seeds and chopped cilantro.

2. Mix the chicken with all the marinating ingredients and let it sit for at least 25 minutes.

3. 4 cups of vegetables that can include Napa cabbage, mushrooms, spinach, and Chinese celery, chop them into bite-sized pieces.

4. In the boiling stock, cook the vegetables for a minute and then remove them. Then cook the glass noodles in the stock and remove them. Place the vegetables and noodles in a bowl.

5. Add the chicken into the simmering broth and cook it for a few minutes until the chicken is done. Also, add in the eggs and stir it until it is cooked.

6. In the bowl, pour the soup and some spoonfuls of sauce.

7. To make a dipping sauce, dilute the suki sauce with sriracha sauce and dip the meat into it before eating. Thai-style sukiyaki is done!

Thai Pumpkin Soup with Shrimp

Thai Pumpkin soup with shrimp is a blissful soup that is rich, creamy, mellow, and appealing to the eyes and the heart. This simple and healthy dish is very similar to the pumpkin soup except in the aspect of flavoring. The thickness of the soup can be perfectly paired with fried prawns that are seasoned with turmeric and coriander powder that takes the soup to the next level, where the dense flavors dance on your taste buds. Check out our detailed instructions to make this smooth and luscious soup!

Ingredients:

- 2 tablespoons of cooking oil
- 1 ½ teaspoons of turmeric powder
- 4 teaspoons of coriander powder
- 10-12 medium-sized de-shelled and deveined prawns
- 2 cups of butternut pumpkin puree
- 1 garlic pod- roasted
- 2 roasted shallots
- 1 stalk of lemongrass- white part crushed
- 2 ½ teaspoons of lime juice
- 2 ½ teaspoons of palm sugar
- 1 teaspoon of fish sauce
- 3 cups of vegetable stock
- 3 teaspoons of miso paste
- 1 ½ tablespoons of finely chopped ginger
- Salt to taste
- Pepper powder to taste
- 1 tablespoon of coconut cream
- 4 sprigs of cilantro for garnish
- 2-4 teaspoons of roasted black sesame seeds for garnish

Preparation time: 1 hour

Serving Size: 4

Instructions:

1. Heat the vegetable stock with lemongrass, palm sugar, and fish sauce and bring it to a boil. After turning off the flame, add the lime juice.

2. Blend the pumpkin puree with roasted garlic and shallots with 1 ½ cup of vegetable stock.

3. Blend again after the addition of miso paste and ginger.

4. In a pan with heated oil, add the prawns, turmeric, and coriander powder and fry them for a few minutes until they are cooked.

5. Add the blended mixture into the pan, add salt and pepper and stir well. Dilute with the vegetable stock if needed. Boil it for 2-3 minutes. Then add the coconut cream and combine it well. Turn off the heat.

6. Pour the soup into a bowl and garnish with cilantro and sesame seeds.

Gai Tom Khamin (Turmeric Chicken Soup)

Southern Thailand is popular for using fresh turmeric in their recipes. Gai Tom Khamin is a delicious soup that will leave you wanting more. This soup is served alongside a homemade spicy condiment Nam Jim that takes the soup's flavor to the next level. This golden soup is easy to make and uses simple ingredients. Add a Thai twist to your chicken soup by following the listed instructions!

Ingredients:

For the soup:

- 3 Pounds of Chicken chopped
- 2 bird's eye chilies
- 6 Cups of Chicken Stock
- 2 stalks of Lemongrass beaten and then sliced
- 3 inches galangal- sliced
- 6 chopped shallots
- 2 of the 2-inches fresh turmeric sliced across the length (be wary of the staining properties of turmeric)
- 4 garlic cloves chopped
- 6 kaffir lime leaves torn to the center- remove the midrib vein
- 2 tablespoons of tamarind juice (then adjust it according to the tanginess required)
- Salt to taste

For the spicy sauce- Nam Jim:

- 6 cloves of Garlic
- 6-7 bird's eye chilies
- 3-4 teaspoons of Fish Sauce
- 3 tablespoons of Lime Juice
- ¼ teaspoon Salt

Preparation time: 45 minutes

Serving Size: 4

Instructions:

1. Pound the garlic, chilies, and salt. Then add fish sauce and lime juice to the coarsely pounded mixture and blend it into a sauce.

2. Add the chicken stock to a pan. Once it starts boiling, turn the heat to low and add the shallots, lemongrass, garlic, turmeric, galangal, and kaffir lime leaves.

3. After it boils for a few minutes, add in the chicken, salt, bird's eye chilies, and tamarind juice.

4. Let the broth simmer for around 30 minutes. During this time, if there is anything floating at the brim, remove it.

5. Serve the soup alongside Nam Jim.

Conclusion

Hopefully, this book has given you insights on Thai food culture, particularly their soups. Now, making a multitude of scrumptious, invigorating, flavorsome, and nutritious soups is no longer a difficult task. You can start making your own versions through combinations of different Thai soups according to your needs and wishes as the recipes are a breeze!

Beat your cravings for a fancy soup with the gratifying easy-to-prepare Thai soup recipes and fill your heart and soul with warm aroma, yummy food, and love!

About the Author

Ivy's mission is to share her recipes with the world. Even though she is not a professional cook she has always had that flair toward cooking. Her hands create magic. She can make even the simplest recipe tastes superb. Everyone who has tried her food has astounding their compliments was what made her think about writing recipes.

She wanted everyone to have a taste of her creations aside from close family and friends. So, deciding to write recipes was her winning decision. She isn't interested in popularity, but how many people have her recipes reached and touched people. Each recipe in her cookbooks is special and has a special meaning in her life. This means that each recipe is created with attention and love. Every ingredient carefully picked, every combination tried and tested.

Her mission started on her birthday about 9 years ago, when her guests couldn't stop prizing the food on the table. The next thing she did was organizing an event where chefs from restaurants were tasting her recipes. This event gave her the courage to start spreading her recipes.

She has written many cookbooks and she is still working on more. There is no end in the art of cooking; all you need is inspiration, love, and dedication.

Author's Afterthoughts

I am thankful for downloading this book and taking the time to read it. I know that you have learned a lot and you had a great time reading it. Writing books is the best way to share the skills I have with your and the best tips too.

I know that there are many books and choosing my book is amazing. I am thankful that you stopped and took time to decide. You made a great decision and I am sure that you enjoyed it.

I will be even happier if you provide honest feedback about my book. Feedbacks helped by growing and they still do. They help me to choose better content and new ideas. So, maybe your feedback can trigger an idea for my next book.

Thank you again

Sincerely

Ivy Hope

Printed in Great Britain
by Amazon

21929353R00057